BECOMING WE

METAMORPHOSIS
AND PEOPLE WITH LEARNING DISABILITIES

David Singer

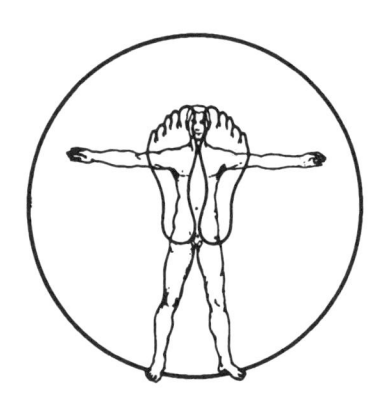

PUBLISHED BY

David Singer,
Flat 2,
53, Silver Street,
TAUNTON
Somerset
TA1 3DL

First edition published in 1993
by Synthesis Publishing

This revised edition published in 1995
by David Singer

This book is dedicated to Jeric.

Copyright © David Singer 1995

Cover illustration by Sarah Arthur
Copyright © Sarah Arthur 1995

All rights reserved

ISBN 0 951 8074 6 3

ABOUT THE AUTHOR

David Singer trained with Gaston Saint-Pierre, founder and director of the Metamorphic Association, in 1988, whilst working as a teacher of children with severe learning disabilities in Somerset. Having observed how some of the children who regularly received sessions of the Metamorphic Technique were very effectively able to move out of old patterns of stress, he began to explore the potential of using the technique with adults.

Since 1990 he has been working extensively as a freelance practitioner for Hampshire Social Services combined with private practice. He now also teaches and lectures throughout the U.K. providing training for staff in the education, health and social services, as well as the public generally.

CONTENTS

List of Illustrations 6

Acknowledgements 7

Forewords by Robert St. John and Gaston Saint-Pierre 8

Introduction 11

1. Communication : A New Starting Point 15

2. Metamorphosis 19

3. History 22

4. The Prenatal Pattern 30

5. Transformation in Practice 33

6. The Practice 44

7. The Practice Illustrated 51

8. Introducing the Practice 65

9. Doing it for Themselves 72

10. Conclusion 78

Further Information 79

LIST OF ILLUSTRATIONS

CHAPTER THREE

1. Chart of the Reflex Zones of the Body 23

2. Reflexes of the Upper Surfaces of the Feet 24

3. Reflexes of the Under Surfaces of the Feet 25

4. Chart of the Prenatal Pattern as Formulated by Robert St. John 28

CHAPTER SIX

5. Chart of the Moving, Doing and Thinking Centres 45

6. Chart of the Foot Relating to the Prenatal Pattern 47

7. Chart of the Prenatal Reflexes of the Hands 49

8. Chart of the Prenatal Reflexes of the Head 50

CHAPTER SEVEN

9–20. The Practice Illustrated 51

CHAPTER NINE

21. Doing it for Oneself 76

ACKNOWLEDGEMENTS

To Robert St. John for discovering Metamorphosis, and for permission to use illustrations from his book *Metamorphosis* (Figs. 2 and 3).

To Gaston Saint-Pierre whose books and training have given me such a thorough understanding of this work and for his constructive criticism of the typescript.

To Mary Lambert for her kind permission to use illustrations from her book *Finding Your Feet* (Figs. 1,4,5,6,7 and 8).

To the Foot Massage Group at Bishopstoke Day Services for their kind permission to take photographs of them which form the basis for some of the illustrations that appear in Chapters 7 and 9 and to Nikki King and Paul Saxton for their assistance with the others (Figs. 9, 15 and 18).

To Jan Cuerdon, Adam Hope, Gill Pettitt, Sharon Smith, Jonathan Everleigh, Adam and Jane Warren, Ed Towers, Simon Chapman, Sarah-Jane Sampson, Charles Le Huquet and Mick Lenehan for all their help along the way. Special thanks to Charlotte Hilton and Liehr.

To the many staff at the establishments I have worked at for recognising the potential of this work and enabling it to become accessible to those who have expressed a genuine need for it, in particular the staff at Selworthy School in Somerset, and Bishopstoke Day Services and Southampton Day Services in Hampshire.

Most of all to everyone who has ever put their feet upon my lap for teaching me the immense value of true individuality.

FOREWORDS

by Robert St. John and Gaston Saint-Pierre

In this book Dave Singer has certainly shown his ability in in both the care of children with learning difficulties, and in his comprehension and handling of Metamorphosis.

I like his direct approach to the subject, his fearlessness in presenting Metamorphosis to medically orthodox people and his very clear explanation of this method and, last of all, his tact with all concerned.

I am looking forward to receiving the finished version of this book and regard it as one of the best publications for the furtherance of Metamorphosis.

~ Robert St. John, October, 1993.

Over the last few years, the Metamorphic Association has gratefully received articles detailing the experiences and observations of Dave Singer, a Metamorphic practitioner. These were published in *Metamorphosis*, the Journal of the Metamorphic Association. It was fascinating to note the range of his activities and through his writing to be able to share in the insights he gained in the field.

In his book he has succeeded in distilling his knowledge while illustrating the wondrous ways in which the innate intelligence of the people with multiple handicaps works. This I feel could not have been achieved without a keen sensitivity and tremendous respect for the people who benefited from his teaching and his presence at their side. This is amply demonstrated in the various approaches to people which Dave Singer describes.

Metamorphosis is deeply rooted in objective love and we could apply to Dave Singer a phrase from T.S. Eliot: "To care and yet not to care". His book is his own testimony to this.

~ Gaston Saint-Pierre, November, 1993.

INTRODUCTION

Whilst working as a teacher at a school for children with severe learning disabilities, it became apparent to me that a lot of the problems that many of the children were experiencing were related to stress. Their capacity to learn and their potential for further growth seemed to be constantly hindered by this factor.

I began to explore various approaches that sought to address this issue of stress. Of all of the approaches, I was most drawn to those involving contact. I had taken on a post at the school where my responsibility was to promote language development and recognised the importance of touch – surely the most basic and fundamental form of human interaction and communication. Its potential value for those with limited abilities to communicate on a verbal level or even a physical level was obvious. But many of the methods available seemed to be rather intrusive or otherwise inappropriate or else posed all sorts of practical problems in applying them in the classroom setting.

One day I came home from a particularly exhausting day at the school and found that my feet were killing me. So, as one does, I prepared a bowl of hot water and soaked my feet. Up until then I had little awareness of my feet, regarding them as being "over there somewhere". I realised then how much I had neglected them and began to apply some lotion to them. It was a reflection perhaps of how much I had neglected and become out of touch with myself but now I was taking responsibility and acknowledging those aspects of myself I had previously failed to take much notice of. Whatever the case, I discovered, much to my surprise, that the act of rubbing feet made me feel deeply relaxed almost immediately.

That this simple act could have such a profound effect made a great impression upon me and it suddenly occurred to me that if rubbing feet could help me to relax then perhaps the children at the school might also benefit from such contact.

My concern however was to introduce such contact in an uninvasive manner and to ensure that the underlying causes of the stress were addressed. It was then that I came across the Metamorphic Technique which adopts the theme of non-interference at a fundamental level. It is a practice which recognises that ultimately we create our own stresses and provides a means of bringing about a permanent resolution at a deeper level through the provision of gentle contact on certain parts of the feet, hands and head.

This book marks the end of a five year period during which I have been exploring the potential of using the Metamorphic Technique with both children and adults with learning disabilities in special schools, day and residential services as a teacher, day service officer and freelance practitioner.

It is primarily aimed at staff and practitioners who work in these fields but it will also be of interest and use to parents and carers, as well as to staff working in other areas of needs–led service provision, including those working with people with physical disabilities, the elderly, people with a mental illness, and children with emotional problems.

The basic principles and practice of the technique are outlined and presented simply and clearly with the aid of illustrations and diagrams. A description of how to give a "standard session" is included and practical issues related to the introduction and use of the technique in the classroom/care setting are fully addressed, based largely upon my own observations and experiences of using it with a variety of individuals and groups in a wide range of different settings. Where appropriate, actual examples are given as an aid to clarifying such issues as well as to elucidate some of the principles involved.

The Metamorphic Technique is a simple and versatile approach to personal growth that is accessible to all and that of course includes people with learning disabilities.

I very much hope that you will thoroughly enjoy sharing this work with those around you.

~ David Singer, Southampton, 1993.

1. COMMUNICATION: A NEW STARTING POINT

Attitudes towards people with learning disabilities have altered radically in recent times, and this is reflected in the many far-reaching changes that have taken place in those services involved in the care, support and education of children and adults.

Children once regarded as "ineducable" are now receiving individualised education in special schools and units and, with appropriate support, many children are now able to attend ordinary schools alongside their peers. Adults, who in the past were placed in large, impersonal and restrictive institutions, are now increasingly able to obtain "needs–led" day and residential services geared towards enabling them to live a more independent life in the community.

Such developments arose out of recognition of the need to move on from the limitations of an "out of sight, out of mind" philosophy in response to a growing awareness that people, no matter what the nature or extent of their learning disability, have the potential to become far more than had previously been considered possible. These substantial advances could not of course have been successfully made without fully acknowledging the sometimes considerable difficulties that people with learning disabilities can experience. However, the predominant theme has been to centre service provision upon the whole person rather than upon his disability alone.

Certainly there is often a great deal that we can do to directly help someone to overcome the obstacles that prevent him from realising his potential, but inevitably there are times when we reach the limits of what we are able to do for another. At worst, we may even find ourselves at a complete loss as to what can be done. This can result in feelings of helplessness or inadequacy, particularly in circumstances where much time and energy has been expended and no real identifiable progress has been achieved. Such situations can be profoundly challenging at both a personal and professional level, for they cause us to question more deeply what the underlying nature of this potential is and how we can best enable it to find expression.

Various theories may be formulated, approaches adopted and programmes implemented but one thing is quite clear, the source of this potential lies within the individual himself, as does the means by which it can begin to actualise, be it in the form of action or communication. Indeed we could say that the problem is primarily one of communication in the broadest sense of the word, since our concern is with those who are experiencing difficulties in expressing their individuality.

For many people with learning disabilities the usual paths of communication have become impeded or blocked in some way. Where communication at a verbal level has become inhibited or distorted then the potential for non–verbal communication needs to be explored, that is, those forms of interaction that occur largely through the medium of the body, such as movement, gesture, facial expression and so on. But there may be a difficulty here also in which case there is a need to operate at another, more basic level.

The simplest and most fundamental form of communication is

surely touch. When offered with appropriate sensitivity, touch can be tremendously reassuring to people who are experiencing difficulty in their lives, because we are able to make actual contact with the person and plainly convey to him that we are here. In this way we acknowledge that "We are together" whilst, at the same time, recognising that "You are you" and "I am me" – the basis upon which all forms of effective communication are founded. So touch can both confirm individuality and transcend the barriers that separate people.

But many children and adults with learning disabilities are apprehensive about touch and are very reluctant to satisfy such a basic human need. In fact, some people can become so overwhelmed by the experience of touch (sometimes even by the anticipation of it) that they become agitated and withdrawn. So an explicitly non–invasive approach is called for that affirms a deep respect for the individual's personal space.

The feet, hands and head are situated at the edge of this space because they lie at the peripheral areas of the body. They are also our main links with the outside world, providing us with the means to make contact and interact with our surroundings. We use our feet to move from one place to another. We use our hands for creative expression and to communicate with each other through touch. In the head are housed the sensory functions of sight, hearing, taste and smell which, together with the brain, help to inform us about the world around us.

The Metamorphic Technique involves the use of unintrusive contact which is applied to certain parts of the feet, hands and head, effectively providing the recipient with a space free of direction and interference. The person is temporarily freed from the demands of communication at the more sophisticated levels, together with their associations with repeated experiences of failure. At the same time, the conditions now exist for the essence of the person to emerge of its own volition, revealing a new starting point from which further communication can develop.

2. METAMORPHOSIS

The main principle underlying this work is that within each of us lies the potential for transformation and this process of radical change can occur naturally and spontaneously given the right conditions. The Metamorphic Technique is essentially a simple way of creating these conditions.

The feet, hands and head are the extremities of the body. By providing a gentle and uninvasive form of contact to these outermost areas, we are being there for the person in a very tangible way whilst, at the same time, conveying an attitude of non-interference.

In so doing, we are creating a space free of direction or external influence within which the recipient is enabled to become sensitised to his or her own inner needs and resources, thereby bringing about the possibility of an improvement at both a physical and psychological level. The emphasis is upon a change from within rather than seeking to impose a change from without. The practice is therefore, in effect, a tool for empowerment.

A light touch is applied to specific areas of the feet, known as the spinal reflex areas, situated along the inside edge of each foot, as well as corresponding areas in the hands and head. The practitioner provides an environment within which deeply-rooted energy blockages may be loosened and released – energy blockages thought to have become established as far back as the gestation period, the nine months we spent in the womb before birth.

What do we mean by energy blockages? When things are not

going well for us, when we feel restricted by our current situation and begin to feel frustrated or depressed by the lack of movement in our lives, we speak of being "stuck in a rut". This expression describes very well the existence of an underlying energy blockage as it affects us in our everyday lives. In the case of the child or adult with learning disabilities, this underlying energy blockage is more profound and its influence is consequently rather more severe.

Conversely, we use the expression "going with the flow" to describe how it feels when our energy (whatever it is that keeps us alive) is flowing freely without hindrance. We tend to regard apparent obstacles or challenges as new opportunities for learning and growth rather than indications of impending disaster or crisis. There is an overall feeling of rightness about what is happening in our lives and a sense of balance in our being. There is a movement towards a more optimum state. In the case of, for example, the autistic child he discovers within himself the capacity to move out of the "prison" of his isolation and begins to interact with his immediate surroundings and those around him.

The energy blockages are "loosened" so that the energy can become free of obstruction. There is no attempt to stimulate, suppress, direct or force the energy in any way whatsoever as this would be to impose an outside influence at the possible expense of the person's own capacity to help and heal himself. The gentle contact provided is indicative of a desire to be of service but also conveys an attitude of detachment, of remaining out of the way and, under these conditions, the full force of the individual's life energy is allowed to flow with complete freedom. The practitioner's role is to act as a catalyst for a movement of change for the better.

This approach does not concern itself with the relief of the symptoms of stress but rather creates the means by which the underlying cause of the stress can reveal itself and transform itself of its own accord. Were we to deal directly with a person's difficulties by soothing away his troubles, he would certainly experience relief and we may feel very pleased that we have produced an instant result. However, the situation is likely to be only temporary whilst the underlying cause remains and thus the symptoms will eventually return once again. They may return in some other form but they will nonetheless eventually return. By working at a more fundamental level, a permanent change can occur because the purpose of the ailments is touched upon and then released.

Viewed from this perspective, the manifestation of a difficulty or problem can be regarded simply as an indication that some aspect of the person is attempting to come into being, but is prevented from doing so because there is a blockage in the free flowing of the person's life–force. By loosening the blockage the way is clear for new growth and development to take place.

The term "Metamorphosis" is used here in the context of personal growth in recognition of the fact that transformation of one's life can occur in a natural way with the necessary energy originating from within the person. For the individual concerned, it involves letting go of old ways of being, thereby freeing him to create a new, quite different life.

3. HISTORY

ZONE THERAPY

The ancient Chinese method of Zone Therapy was rediscovered by Dr. William Fitzgerald, an American doctor, who brought it to the attention of the medical world in 1914.

He found that there exist in the body 10 longitudinal zones which run from the top of the head to the tips of the fingers and toes; each organ of the body was located in one or more of these sections *(see Fig. 1)*. His investigations confirmed that, by massaging a finger or toe situated at the end of these zones, a definite effect occurs in bringing about the normal physiological functioning in all parts of the body reflected in the corresponding zone, resulting from an activation of energy flow throughout the area concerned.

RELEXOLOGY

This work was taken a step further during the 1930s by another American, Eunice Ingham, who developed the practice that is today known as Reflexology. It was subsequently introduced into Britain during the 1960s by Doreen Bayley.

Reflexology is based upon the principle that the feet mirror or reflect the whole body *(see Figs. 2 and 3)*. By massaging specific areas of the feet, harmony and balance can be restored to the corresponding parts of the body through stimulating a flow of energy.

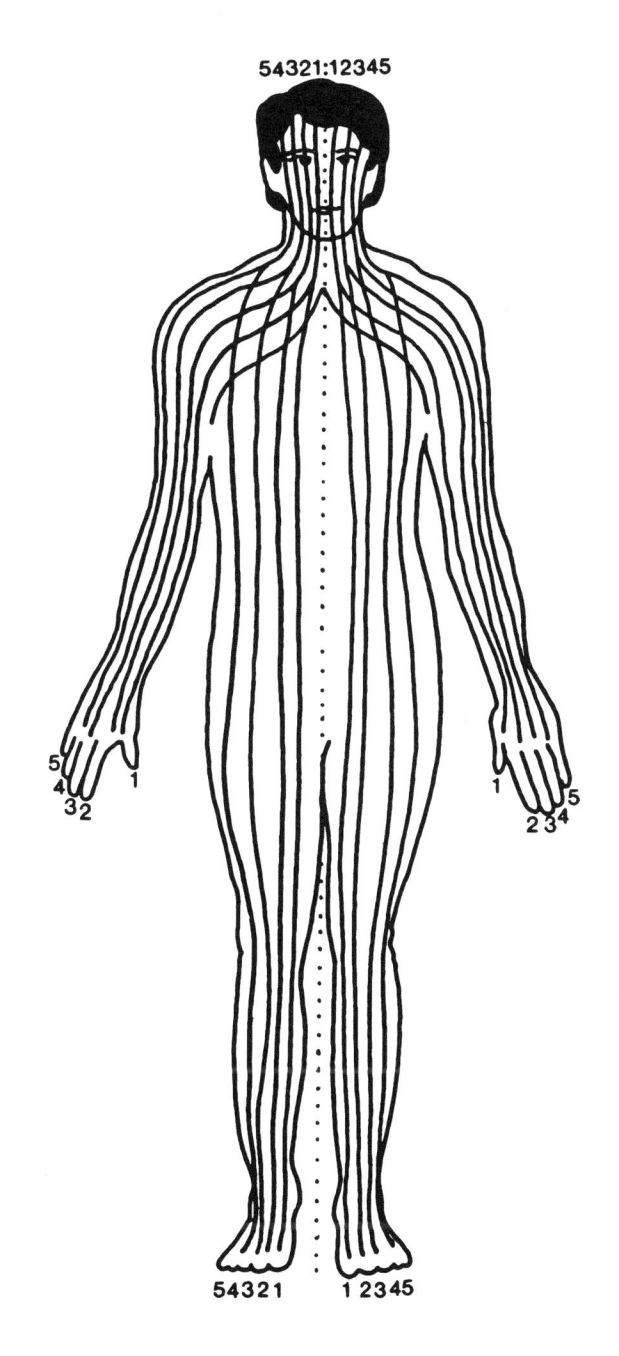

1 Chart of the reflex zones of the body

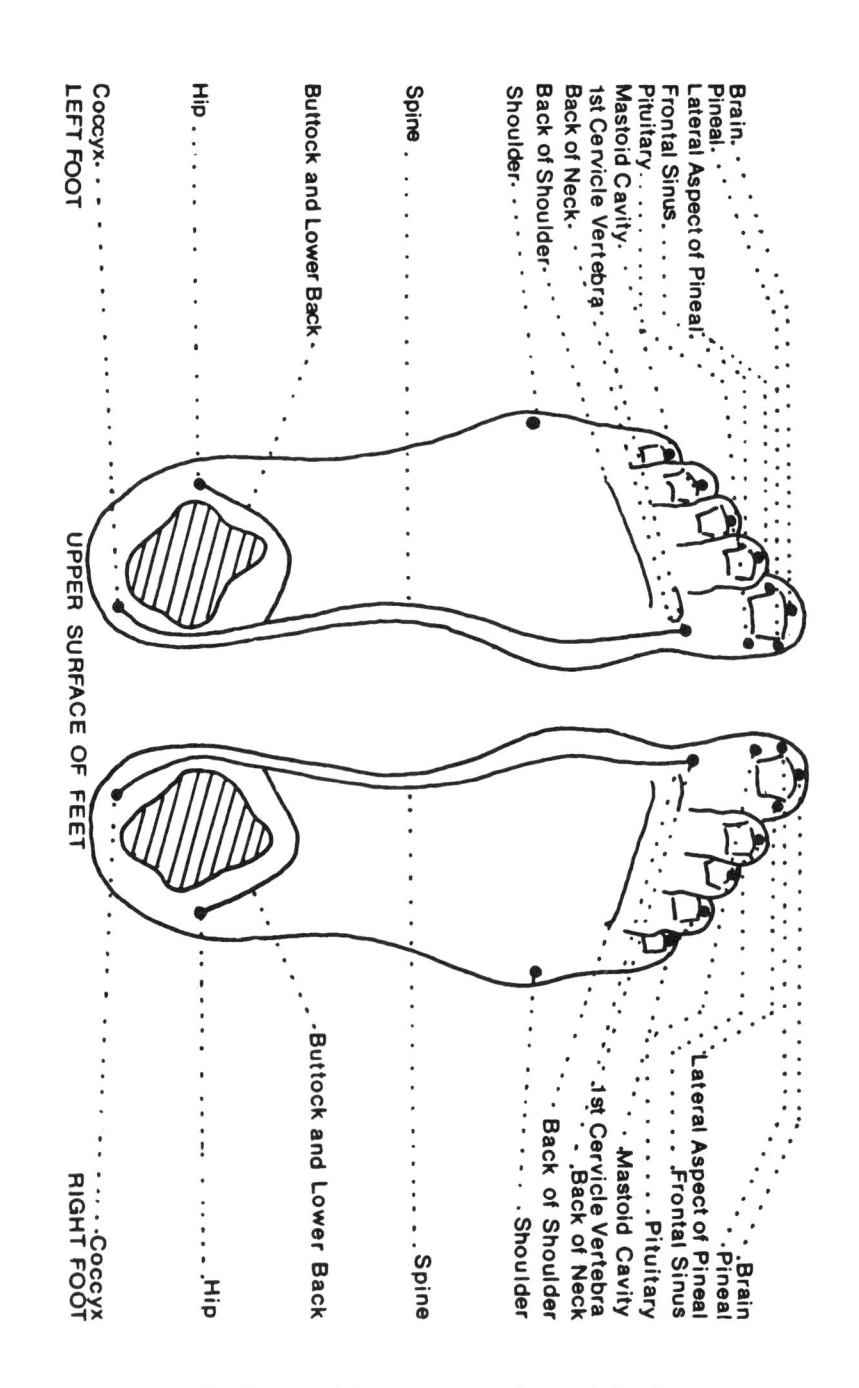

2 *Reflexes of the upper surface of the feet*

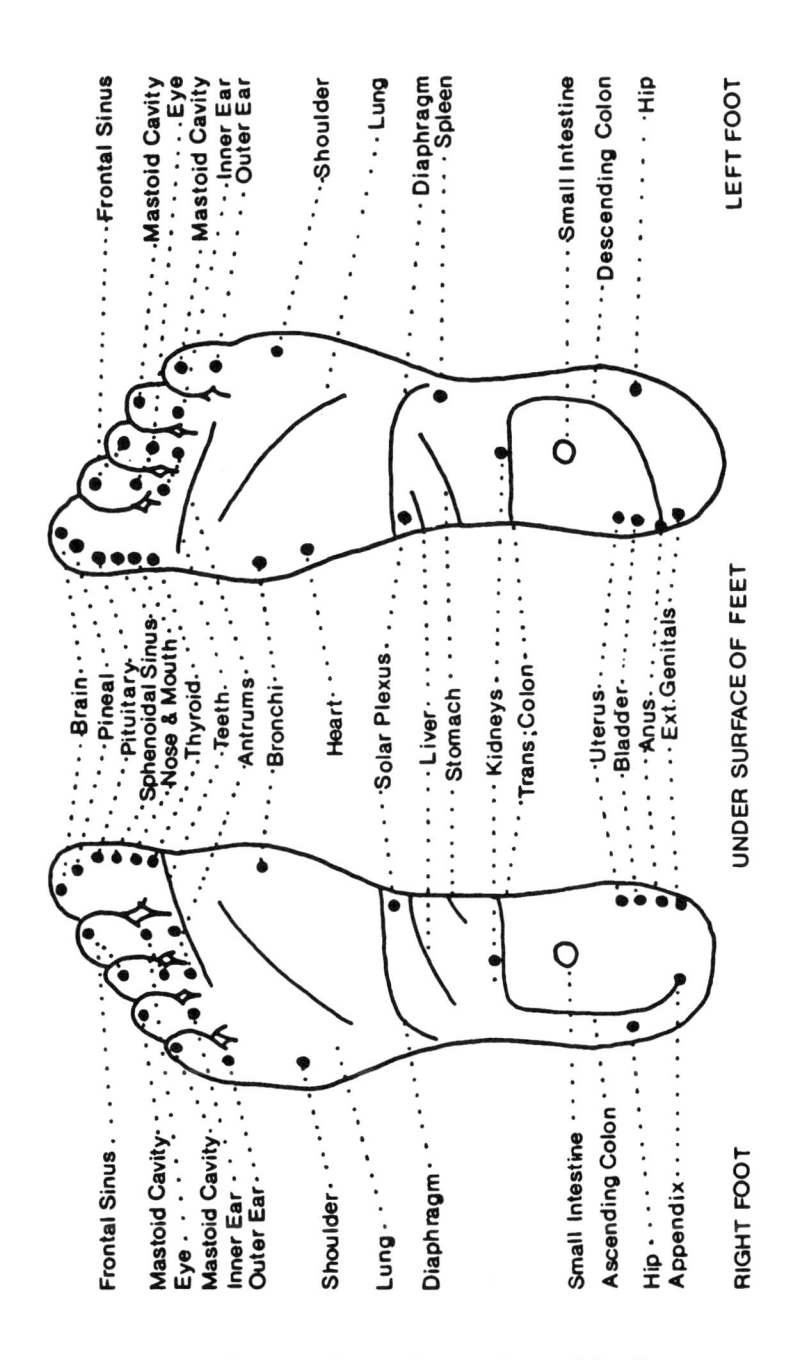

3 Reflexes of the under surface of the feet

PRENATAL THERAPY

Robert St. John, a British naturopath, evolved the practice of Prenatal Therapy during the 1960s based upon the principles of Reflexology.

He had become dissatisfied with natural therapeutic practices of the time because he felt that they did not recognise that the causative factors responsible for illness ultimately stem from within the individual. At some level, he proposed, we create our own stresses which in turn have an adverse effect at both a physical and psychological level.

Whilst exploring the potential of treatment through the feet, he discovered that physical illnesses corresponded to a blockage in the reflex area of the spine. By confining treatment to these specific areas, the same results were produced rendering it unnecessary to work on the other zones of the feet.

Recognising the importance of the connection between the mind and the body, he began to turn his attention to the psychological aspects of the treatment.

He found that there was a correspondence between the heel area of the spinal reflexes and what he termed as the maternal principle. A blockage here manifested itself at a psychological level as a difficulty in the person's relationship with his mother, in being a mother, or in the capacity to nourish, nurture or care for others or for oneself. Later, it was found to also indicate a difficulty in the person's ability to be grounded.

Such blockages were indicated by the appearance of, for example, an area of callused skin. As the blockage was resolved, so these conditions on the feet disappeared (e.g. an area of hard skin on the heel would return to its usual healthy state).

He identified a correspondence between the first joint of the big toe and the father principle. A blockage here revealed a difficulty in the individual's relationship with his father/boss/person in authority or in being a father. It was subsequently found to also indicate a difficulty in the person's capacity to express his own inner authority.

He discovered later that the spinal reflex points situated along the line connecting these two points between the big toe and the heel also reflected the nine months of the gestation period from the moment of conception to the time of birth *(see Fig. 4.)*. He concluded that the patterns of stress formed during this time continue to exert an influence upon how we are in our present lives since this is a formative period when all our characteristics – physical, mental, emotional and behavioural – are established.

This discovery meant that whereas in Relexology the stresses of the body could be released through the manipulation of the feet, it was possible to release energy blockages established during the prenatal period by working along the spinal reflex points, hence the name Prenatal Therapy.

In order to find a way of enabling the individual to effect permanent changes for the better, it required broadening his perspective beyond the physical and psychological levels. He consequently recognised that all stress and illness ultimately originate from an unconscious attachment to the past, the source of which goes back to the beginnings of life itself.

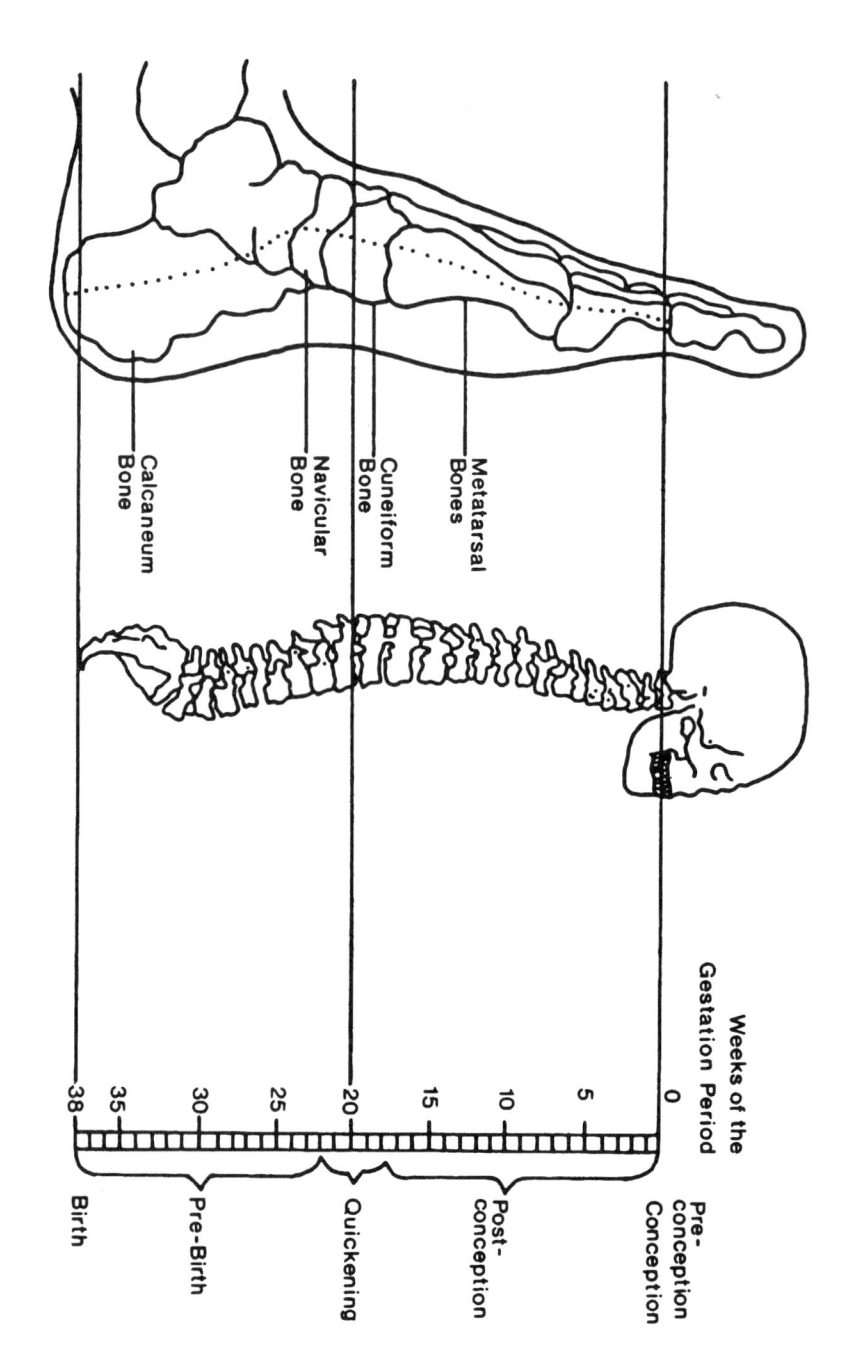

4 Chart of the prenatal pattern as formulated by Robert St. John

METAMORPHOSIS

Robert St. John later referred to this work as "Metamorphosis" in recognition of the fact that radical and far-reaching changes can occur in a natural way, originating from within the individual, through its application.

The term "The Metamorphic Technique" was subsequently coined by Gaston Saint-Pierre who became a student of Robert St. John in 1977, and who set up the Metamorphic Association, a registered charity, in 1979 to promote this work worldwide.

4. THE PRENATAL PATTERN

Robert St. John began treating children with learning disabilities in the mid-1950s and it was this area of his work in particular that contributed to his understanding of the factors that prevent the individual from realising his full potential. It led on to his discovery of Metamorphosis.

He identified the existence of two dynamic and co-existing patterns that exert an influence upon the way we are and he proposed that it is the dominance of one of these patterns that gives rise to stress and illness. On the one hand the individual may withdraw and hold back from life (the Afferent pattern) and, on the other hand, the individual may thrust too forcibly into it (the Efferent pattern). Robert St. John noticed that these tendencies are exhibited in the extreme in the case of the autistic child and the Down's Syndrome child respectively. The autistic child tends to be very reserved, overly hesitant in his approach to new activities and decidedly reluctant to become involved with other people. In contrast, the Down's Syndrome child tends to a very open, highly sociable person who is exceedingly keen to explore new opportunities.

Robert St. John came to realise that these patterns in their unbalanced form become established during the prenatal period. It was evident that the first half of this period with its emphasis upon inwardly-directed growth reflected the Afferent pattern, whilst the second half of this period with its emphasis upon outwardly-directed development reflected the Efferent pattern.

From the moment of **Conception** *(see Fig. 4., page 28)* and during the first four-and-a-half months of the prenatal period (**Post-Conception**), the growth of the embryo and the foetus is focussed upon establishing itself as an independent individual. It is a time when the lungs are formed for example. About halfway through the prenatal period there is a shift from inward growth to outward exploration and development (**Quickening**) – a time when the mother often first feels the foetus move in the womb. During the final four-and-a-half months, the foetus commences preparations for life in the world outside beyond the secure confines of the womb. During this stage (**Pre-Birth**), the beginnings of the qualities of interaction and communication start to emerge as the foetus starts to explore and become aware of its surroundings. This whole process of growth and development culminates in the moment of **Birth** – a time of great change which will determine the person's response later in life when confronted with radical change.

Later he concluded that these patterns originally precipitated at the time of conception when such influences as genetic inheritance and other less easily defined non-material influences come into play.

This unique approach to personal growth developed out of a desire to discover a means of enabling the person to effect permanent changes for the better at both a physical and psychological level, and to find a way of doing so that encompasses the needs of children and adults with learning disabilities.

To be of genuine use to the reader, however, such an approach needs to demonstrate not only its effectiveness as a tool for personal growth, but also its capability of being integrated into the day-to-day reality of providing support to people with learning disabilities in the context of current service provision. These practical issues will be addressed in the following chapters.

5. TRANSFORMATION IN PRACTICE

The Metamorphic Technique is so named because it can bring about a radical change, a transformation, within the individual in a natural and spontaneous way. It is a phenomenon that can occur not only in the individual but in a group context too.

There follow some examples of the kinds of changes that I have observed in both individuals and groups whilst using the technique. The intention behind the use of these examples is neither to raise expectations nor to make claims but simply to illustrate how the underlying principles of this work operate in practice and to give some idea of the potential of this work in these or similar settings.

The most noticeable thing about this practice is that the majority of people who request sessions find the experience very relaxing and enjoyable. For some, this is a big step in itself, for it may be the first time that they have ever sat down for more than a few minutes.

When I first started to use the technique, I was working with a class of six students with high support needs aged between 14 and 19. This was a particularly unsettled and demanding group comprising individuals with enormously different needs. It was obvious that little, if any, teaching and learning could occur under these conditions until the underlying problem of stress had been addressed.

Rather than exhausting ourselves by constantly rushing around and *doing* things for the group, we recognised that there was a need to spend time simply *being* with the students. So, we decided that each week we (myself, the class teacher, and care assistant) would all sit down with the group on mats in one corner of the classroom listening to relaxation music for 10–15 minutes. Gradually we introduced contact on the feet and later the Metamorphic Technique. The group thoroughly enjoyed these sessions and, after several weeks, these sessions began to last for up to 45 minutes.

Most became much more settled. With some, eye contact became noticeably more lucid. They were more present, relating more directly to those around them and their surroundings. It was reported that one hyperactive girl had started to sleep throughout the night, much to the surprise of the home carer concerned. As members of staff, the sessions offered us a way of being with the students without giving rise to feelings of helplessness and inadequacy.

This tendency among recipients to become more settled and relaxed is a common one which can subsequently be followed by a release of energy that can lead to some far-reaching changes.

For example, in the same school, I was asked to help set up a weekly relaxation session for a class of around eight children aged between 6 and 8 years. Once again contact on the feet and later the Metamorphic Technique was introduced by all the staff. The same process occurred. The children became much more settled and the sessions proved to be popular with both staff and pupils.

After a number of weeks, a dramatic change occurred. Quite suddenly one child switched off the relaxation music and pulled out all the jig-saws from a cupboard, then another pulled story books off a book shelf, another stood on top of a table and then the headmistress arrived with a visitor!

Such changes directly challenged our professional roles and the class teacher became quite anxious about the purpose of the session. However, things became clearer once we had acknowledged our own changes – two of us were shortly to move to different towns, another to change jobs (it is a curious phenomenon that those who provide sessions also tend to experience changes in their lives which can sometimes be quite radical). We soon recognised that what in fact was occurring was positive and exciting. The children were setting up learning situations to facilitate their growth. They were not only highly motivated to learn but were actually initiating the learning process. The sessions continued to develop in this new form until the end of term.

It was particularly interesting to observe how the children had become aware of their actual inner needs, rather than being dependent upon those acting upon assumptions about what those needs should be. At the same time they were creating the means by which such surfacing needs could be met. As members of staff, despite the rapid and radical nature of the changes that occurred, the form of our new roles had soon become clear and purposeful.

It is worth examining this particular example further because it reveals much about the nature of transformation itself.

Metamorphosis involves a radical change of form and the energy required to bring about such a change comes from within the individual (or group). All that is necessary to facilitate this process is the existence of a catalyst.

Prior to the sessions the children were very much dependent upon the teaching staff to determine their needs and to create structured teaching sessions to meet those needs as they perceived them. At the time this was a perfectly valid approach given that the children lacked the ability to learn without such support. The important thing to note here is that the motivation for the learning process came largely from the staff who initiated and sustained it through prompting and encouragement.

During the sessions however, the motivation for learning began to emerge quite spontaneously from within the children themselves. Consequently, the whole educational approach needed to change in order to accommodate this shift in the motivational aspect of the learning process. But how did this shift actually occur?

By providing sessions, we were acting as catalysts by effectively loosening the child's grip on the past and its associated influences upon his current way of being. It has already been seen in the previous chapter that such influences, in principle, become established during the formative nine months of the gestation period. It is this hold onto the prenatal period (operating at an unconscious level) that is loosened through this work.

By enabling the child to release his grip on the past, energy that was bound up in sustaining the old way of being becomes available for the creation of an entirely new way of being, hence the release of energy and the new-found motivation. This can happen instantaneously (as in the above example) but more often it tends to occur over a period of time.

The old pattern gave rise to the need for particular forms/structures/approaches and, as a new pattern emerged, then so too did the need for new forms/structures/approaches become apparent.

Both current theories of group dynamics and our own commonsense inform us that when one individual in a group changes then this will, to a greater or lesser degree, have an effect upon all of the other members of that group. This "knock-on" effect occurs whether it be in the case of a group that meets once a week or a closely-knit family. Clearly, the more closely and deeply connected the group, the more profound the impact is likely to be.

Involvement by members of the group concerned in the giving and receiving of sessions enables the group as a whole to handle the impact of such changes creatively. In the case of the above example, the sessions provided us, as members of staff, with the opportunity to "take a step back" from our usual ways of responding thereby enhancing the transformational process. We were more readily able to trust that the growth process which, whilst admittedly looking chaotic for a moment, was in fact bringing about a far more evolved situation than had existed previously.

Having observed this marked increase in awareness in the individual of their own needs and the inner resources to meet those needs, it occurred to me that the Metamorphic Technique might also have a contribution to make in the facilitation of needs-led services for adults with learning disabilities.

After making this practice available to individuals and groups at several day centres and homes for a number of years, I have observed that those receiving sessions will often initiate, or become open to, changes in their day service provision and/or residential situation.

Such changes can be immediate and obvious, such as, in the case of one woman who, as soon as her session was over, went outside to join a gardening group for the first time. Sometimes people will bring about a more fundamental change in their service provision as they become aware of their changing needs. Such changes can initially involve a marked regressive period before a movement forward can occur.

For example, one woman in her thirties (who also had a physical disability), requested to receive sessions on a regular basis which she very much enjoyed. But, after a number of weeks, she began to get increasingly dependent and apparently lacked the motivation to be responsible for herself, much to the understandable frustration of her keyworker. It transpired that her home situation was becoming increasingly difficult to handle – she lived with a home carer and two other residents one of whom she found to be very irritating. She also began to temporarily experience pains in her arms which was making her sharply aware of her physical disability.

After receiving further sessions, there was a sudden movement forward. She expressed a desire to attend a day centre for people with physical disabilities for part of the week (as well as continuing to go to the day centre she was already attending) which she felt was better placed to develop her interest in the particular craft activities she was interested in and also enabled her to broaden her current social life. She also requested to move house. This was brought about in the ensuing weeks, and moreover, she now uses public transport to attend both day centres whereas before she was dependent upon transport being provided for her. This example also demonstrates how inner changes can lead to a change in environment.

People can sometimes experience a temporary period of disorientation or confusion following a session as they accommodate and integrate the inner changes taking place in their everyday life. Such feelings can last from a few minutes to up to one or two days. But it has been observed that, no matter how great the changes, the individual will always find that they can handle them because the release of energy occurs in proportion to the capacity of the individual to handle it. It is a natural release, one that has not been forced. Whilst what manifests on the surface may initially prove challenging, the underlying change is always for the better.

Those who have a genuine desire to change tend to respond more readily to this work. By requesting a session in the first place, the individual is openly acknowledging the need for change in his life. He has gone as far as he can with what he has got and now wishes to go further. What he requires is the means by which he can reassess his needs as necessary and tap into whatever else he has got in the way of inner resources so that he can once again progress. The Metamorphic Technique offers him a way of doing just that.

In general I have noticed that children tend to experience a greater pace of change than adults, which should not be surprising as adults have often been dependent upon others for up to thirty, forty or fifty years. The underlying patterns of stress have had a chance to become more fixed in the adult, whereas they are still flexible in the case of children, who tend to have a greater capacity to step out of these patterns which have only been established for a relatively short time and are less deeply entrenched.

Often the changes that occur appear to be very subtle and barely noticeable from week to week, and it is not until after several weeks or even months that the full extent of the resultant changes becomes evident. Frequently during these times I have wondered if the individual is deriving any benefit. But it is always obvious that they are highly motivated to receive sessions and that they clearly find them relaxing and enjoyable.

For example, one man began to request sessions on a weekly basis during a period when he was going into respite care at weekends away from the parental home – a change that was giving rise to much distress. It was a change that was necessary because his parents were acknowledging that they were no longer able to maintain the level of support that he required due to their advanced years.

One week he chose not to have his feet done which surprised me because up until then he had been very keen to receive sessions on a regular basis. The following week he began to come for sessions again. It transpired that the week he did not attend coincided with the week when he stayed with his parents for an occasional full week. It was evident therefore that he was using the sessions to enable him to handle the changes that were occurring in his life.

Many people request sessions during difficult times, often when experiencing emotional problems associated with the transition from a life of dependency to one of increased self-reliance, such as when moving from the parental home or at a time of bereavement.

Changes in patterns of dependency are a very common occurrence in those who receive sessions regularly as they become sensitised not only to their own needs but also to their inner resources.

Sometimes clients will come to sessions in a profound state of dependency or helplessness. After a number of weeks or months, this begins to change. Rather than seeing themselves as "victims of circumstance", they begin to initiate definite changes in their lives, where necessary making creative use of available facilities and support. There is a shift from reacting to circumstances and situations, to acting to bring about a change based upon the foundation of their own true selves.

I have observed that a few people with physical disabilities do become more mobile, which either occurs quite spontaneously or they begin to make positive use of available support such as physiotherapy, leading to increased mobility.

This does not occur with everyone but, even in these cases, the individuals, rather than feeling imprisoned by the limits of their disability, often tend to initiate changes within those limitations. A new positivity enters the picture as it were.

For example, one very determined woman who was very aware of her difficulty in walking persevered with regular physiotherapy sessions to ensure she kept mobile. But she also came to recognise her limits, and having gained control of her Disability and Mobility Allowance, decided to invest in a "scooter" so that she could go to the local post office and shops.

This shift from helplessness to empowerment can sometimes be quite marked and sudden.

For example, one woman who attended a "foot massage" group at a day centre for adults with learning disabilities (who had a visual impairment and hearing difficulty), used to require a great deal of support to get from her base room to the room where the group session was being held at the other end of the building. At the end of the session, after having had her feet done by a fellow client, she stood up boldly and said "Right then, I'm off!" and, picking up her handbag, proceeded to take herself back to her base room alone.

However, apparently very small changes can reveal a major shift of attitude in people as they get in touch with their inner selves and begin to value their personal power. I am always far more impressed by such changes.

To observe someone with multiple handicaps or a very withdrawn person put his foot out who was previously extremely reticent and fearful of such contact, is not only a very humbling experience for the practitioner, but it is also to witness a major change that has arisen from the very core of that person's being.

For the individual concerned, it can mark the end of a prolonged or even life-long period of isolation, of complete loss of power, and the beginning of the creation of a new life of ever-broadening horizons.

And this is what Metamorphosis is all about. It is about letting go. And as one lets go of how one used to be, energy is released, together with the opening up of possibilities for positive and creative change. This is as true for people with learning disabilities as much as for anyone else.

6. THE PRACTICE

The Metamorphic Technique involves the provision of contact on the feet, hands and head.

Work on the feet brings about a movement of change in the person. Work on the hands enables the person to handle the changes that take place and work on the head helps the person to understand and make sense of what is happening in his life *(see Fig. 5)*.

It is generally recommended that work on the feet does not exceed one hour per week because otherwise this can lead to too much change resulting in feelings of confusion. This does not however apply to children. The hands and head can be worked on for as long and as often as the individual wishes.

WORK ON THE FEET

Start by seating yourself at right angles to the person who wishes to receive a session, with their right foot resting on a small towel or cushion placed upon your lap.

We position ourselves like this in order to convey an attitude of non-interference. In this way, we remain "out of the way". It would be difficult to remain uninvolved if we were to sit opposite the person. We adopt an attitude of detachment throughout the session for two reasons:

Firstly, to ensure that we do not unwittingly interfere with or

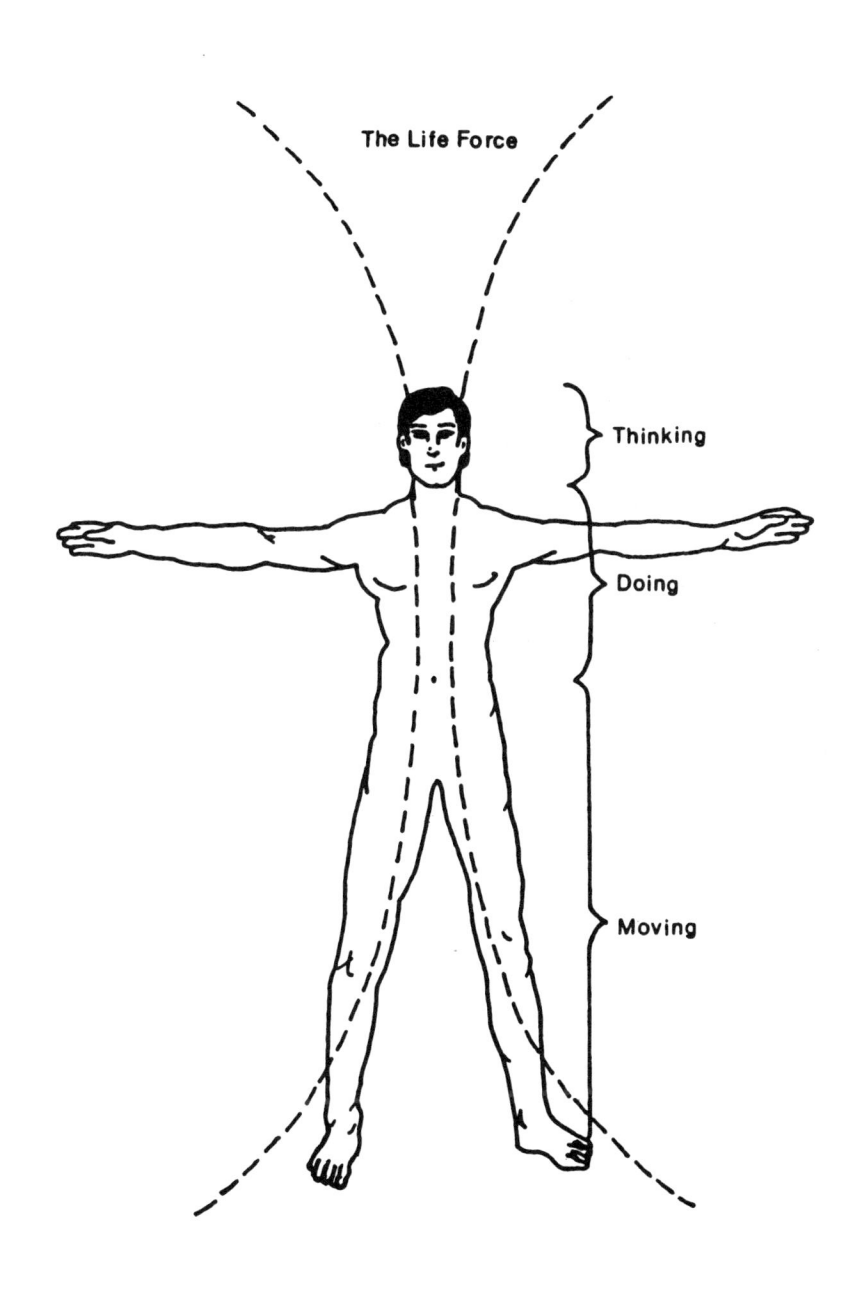

5 *Chart of the moving, doing and thinking centres*

hinder the natural healing and growth process that is facilitated by this contact. Although a session is usually a relaxing experience, we do not aim to relieve tension. Nor do we seek to counsel, guide or advise the individual although we must of course listen attentively and with compassion and allow ourselves to become aware of his difficulties and problems. But rather than trying to change the person in a particular way, by doing this work we are enabling the person himself to change (for the better).

Secondly, very sensitive people can sometimes pick up pains and tensions from the person they are working with. By remaining detached, we do not take on the burden of the person's stresses.

The session can be given on a sofa. If you use chairs ensure that you, as the practitioner, sit on a chair without arms, if possible, so that you can work freely and without restriction. Sometimes it may be more convenient to work on mats on the floor, particularly if you are working with young children or people with multiple handicaps. A session can also be given to someone sitting in a wheelchair or lying on a bed. It makes no difference so long as, if possible, the practitioner is positioned at right angles to the client and you are both comfortable.

We start with the right foot because this is said to reflect what is going on in the person's life at the present time; the left foot reflects what is in potential. This "right foot first" rule is not a hard and fast one though, so do not impose it should the client insist on the left foot being done first. In practice, for example, it has been noticed that hyperactive children tend to ask for the left foot to be worked on first.

Before starting, it is a good idea for you to spend a moment to get centred by putting aside all thoughts of the day. Take the foot firmly in both hands. Allow your hands to move over the whole foot. A firm touch does away with any sense of ticklishness. Let your hands work over the whole foot, the top of the foot, the ankles, the sole, the toes and the heel.

Then, by using your fingers and thumbs, begin working gently up and down the spinal reflex areas from the big toe to the heel *(see Fig. 6)*. The spinal reflex areas run in a line from the side of the big toe, along the bony ridge on the inside of the foot, under the ankle and end at the heel (because the reflexes are more difficult to locate here you can work all over the padded area at the side of the heel). Pay attention also to the reflex areas situated at the corners of the nail of the big toe.

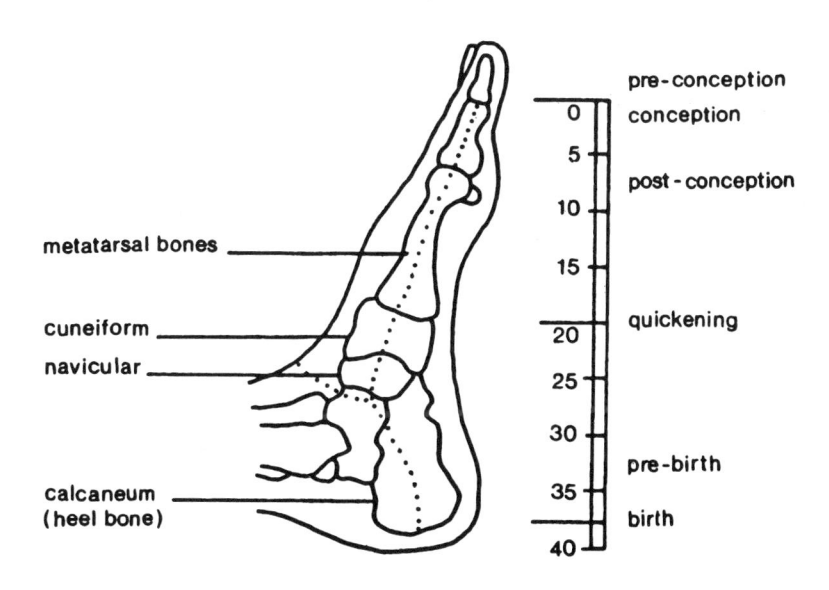

6 Chart of the foot relating to the prenatal pattern

Use any finger you wish with any movement or pressure you feel comfortable with. Allow your fingers to move spontaneously. You can use a circular movement, or a vibratory movement or you can let your fingers glide back and forth. Simply do whatever feels right. From time to time, work across the instep.

During a session, some practitioners experience the need to yawn, sneeze, sigh or burp. Do not suppress these feelings but encourage them as they are a sign that energy is being released. You may find a tingling sensation going up your arms while you are working or find your hands getting heavy; this is also energy being released by the person receiving the session. Shake your arms if this happens so that it does not go into your body. You may experience a feeling of fatigue. In this case, there is a need to ensure that you are centred. Some people experience these symptoms, others don't.

You may work on the feet for up to 20–30 minutes before proceeding onto the next foot. Finish by rubbing the foot all over again then gradually ease your hands away from the foot.

Afterwards, wash your hands under the cold water tap.

WORK ON THE HANDS

Begin by taking the client's right hand and placing it on a small towel or cushion upon your lap. Make sure that you are both comfortable.

Then work in the same way as you did on the feet, beginning at the top of the outer edge of the thumb, working down to the base and across the back of the wrist *(see Fig. 7)*. Continue for 5–10 minutes. Finish by stroking the side of the thumb a few times and gradually ease your hands away from the client's. Then proceed to work on the other.

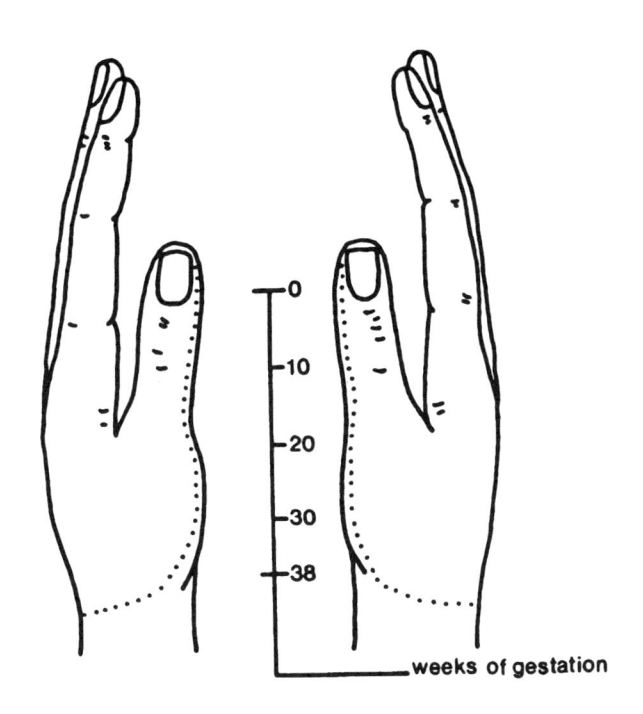

7 Chart of the prenatal reflexes of the hand

WORK ON THE HEAD

To work on the head, you need to be able to stand behind your client. Support the forehead with one hand and gently work with the fingers of the other hand in a light movement as before.

Work from the centre of the top of the head down to the nape of the neck and across the base of the skull and up to the top of the ears *(see Fig. 8)*. You can do this for 5–10 minutes.

Ensure that the movement is very gentle. It should not cause the head to move or tug the hair.

Finish off by gently easing your hand away from the client's head. If you wish you can touch the client's shoulder lightly to let them know that you are finished.

Some people will go into a deeply relaxed state by the end of the session. If so, leave them undisturbed. They will usually come out of it after a few minutes.

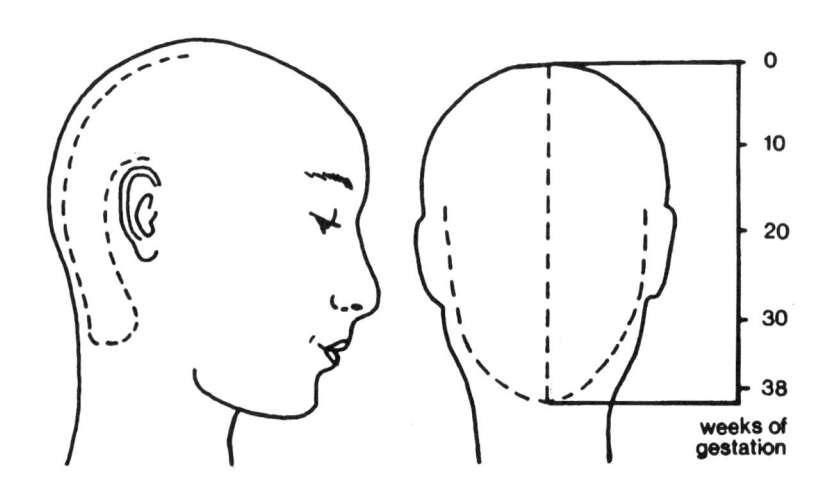

8 Chart of the prenatal reflexes of the head

7.THE PRACTICE ILLUSTRATED

WORK ON THE FEET

9. Start by seating yourself at right angles to the person who wishes to receive a session, with their right foot resting on your lap.

*10 Take the foot firmly in both hands.
Allow your hands to move over the whole foot.*

11 Then, by using your fingers and thumbs, begin working up and down the spinal reflexes from the big toe to the heel.

12 Pay attention also to the reflex areas situated at the corners of the nail of the big toe.

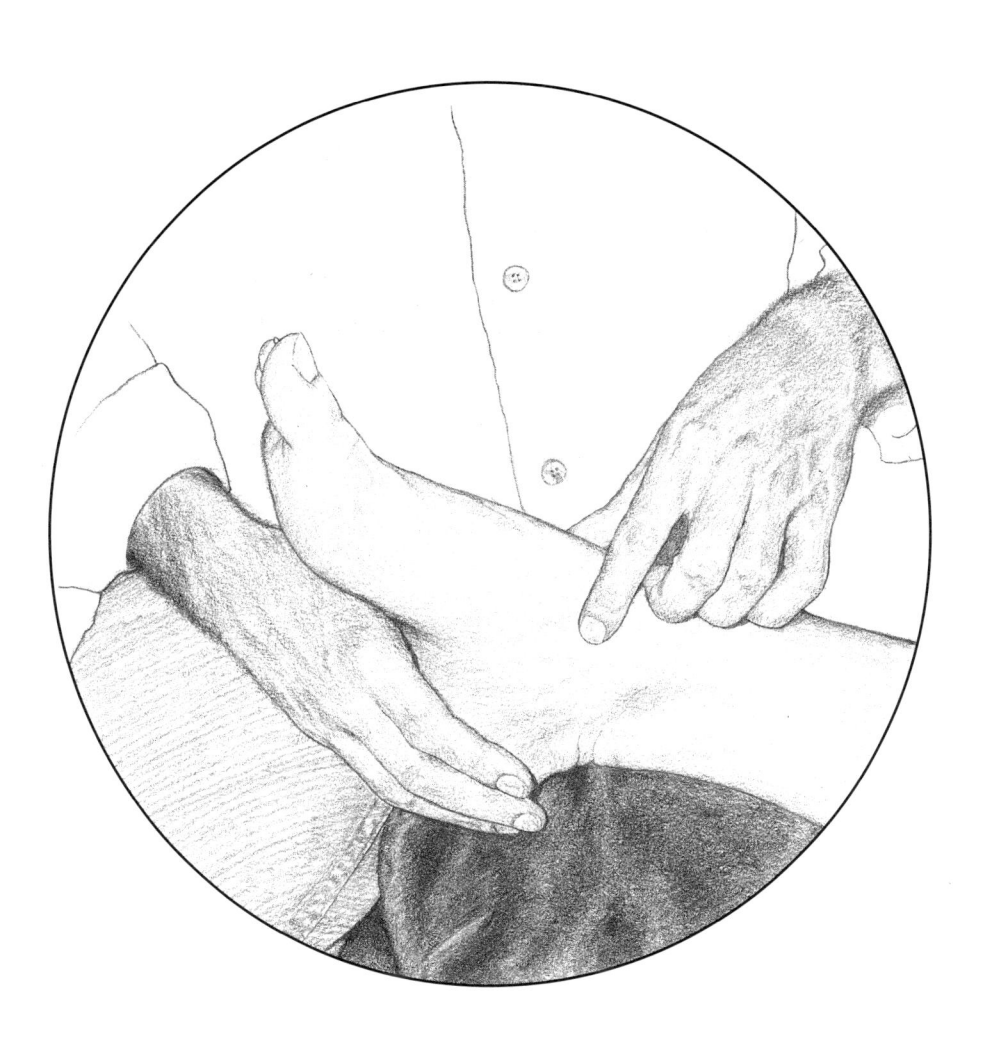

13 From time to time, work across the instep.

14 Finish by rubbing the foot all over again a few times...before proceeding onto the other foot (up to 20–30 minutes on each foot).

WORK ON THE HANDS

15   Begin by taking the client's right hand...

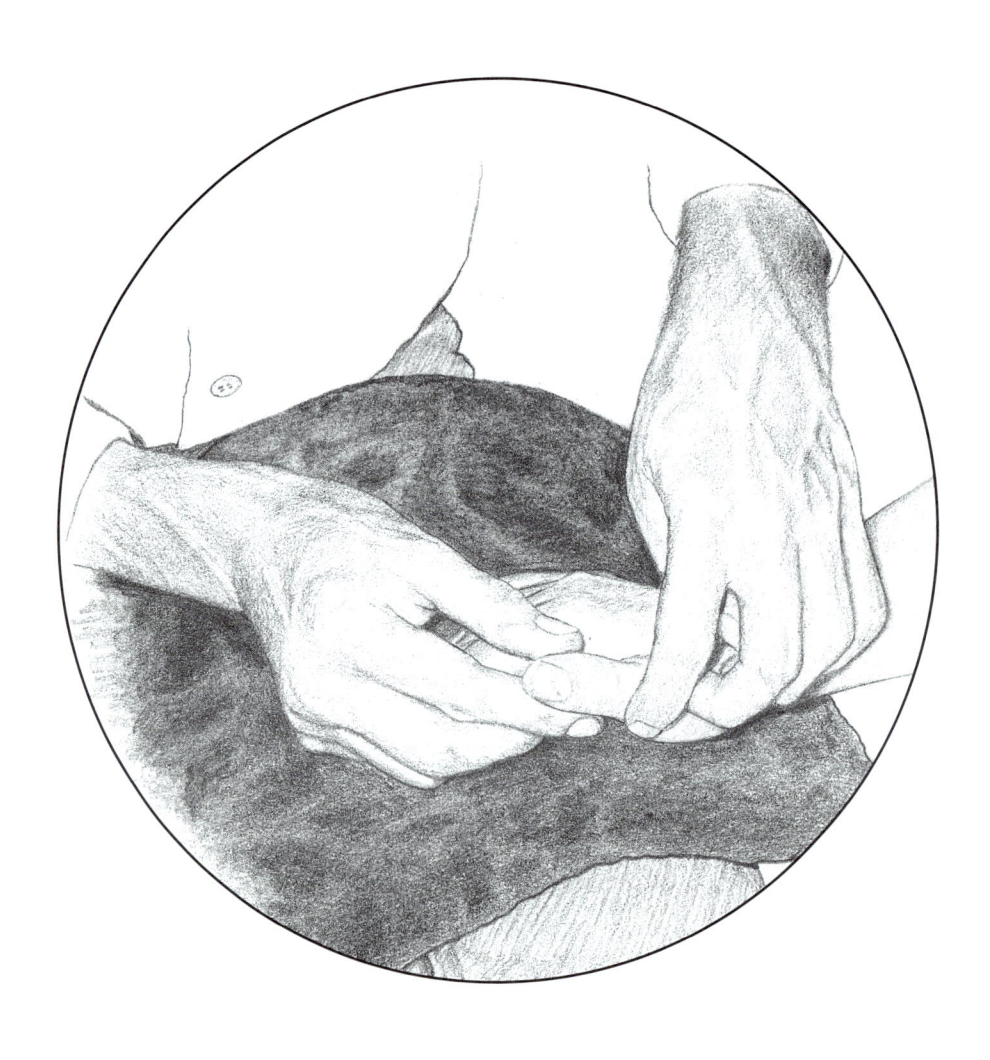

16 ...then work in the same way as you did on the feet, beginning at the top of the outer edge of the thumb, working down to the base ...

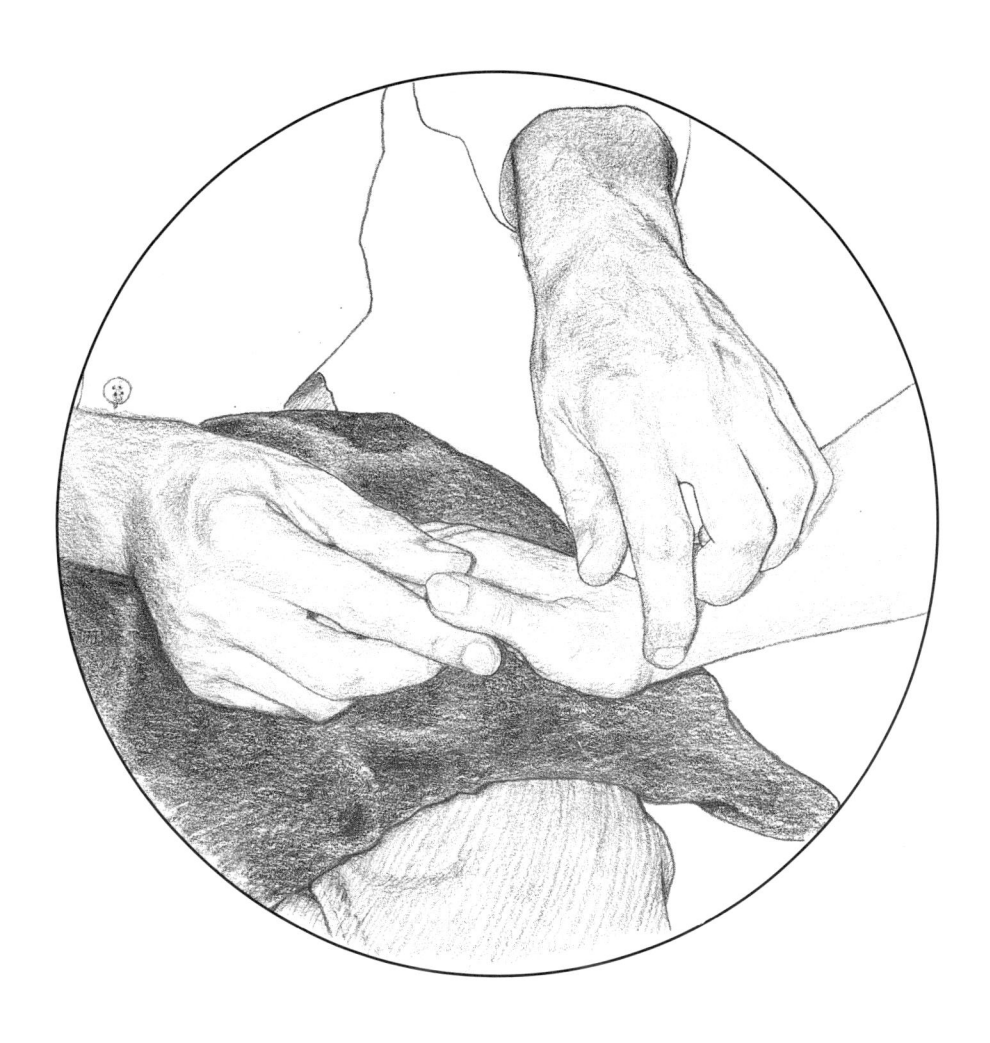

17 ...and across the back of the wrist. Finish by stroking the side of the thumb a few times...then proceed to work on the other (5–10 minutes or longer).

WORK ON THE HEAD

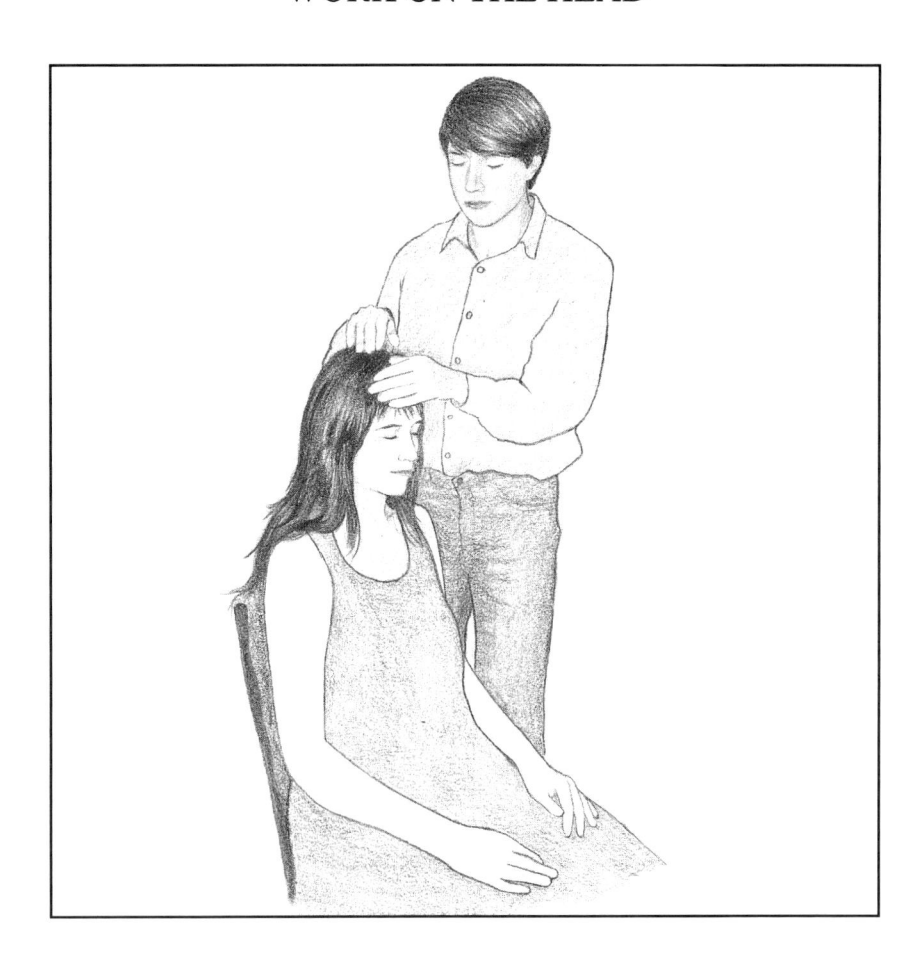

18 Stand behind your client. Support the forehead with one hand.

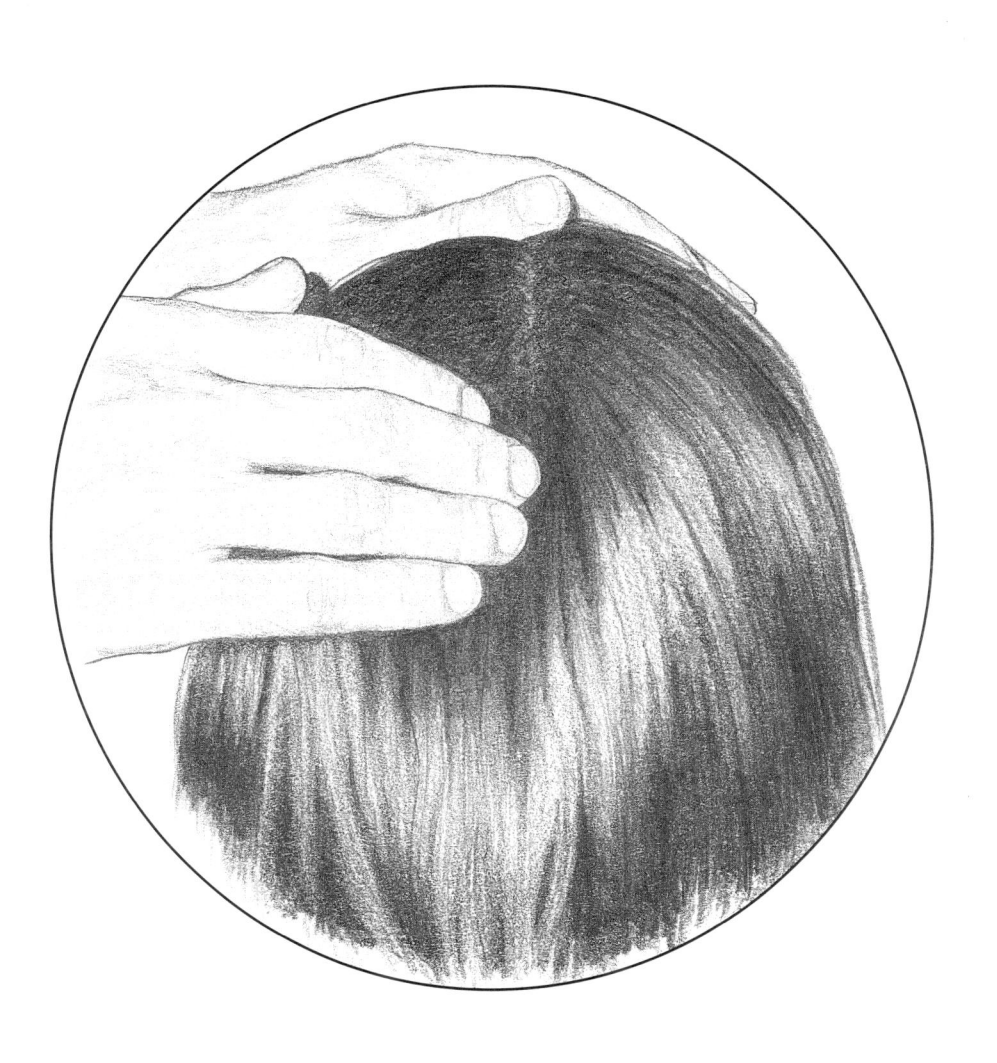

19 Work from the centre to the top of the head down to the nape of the neck...

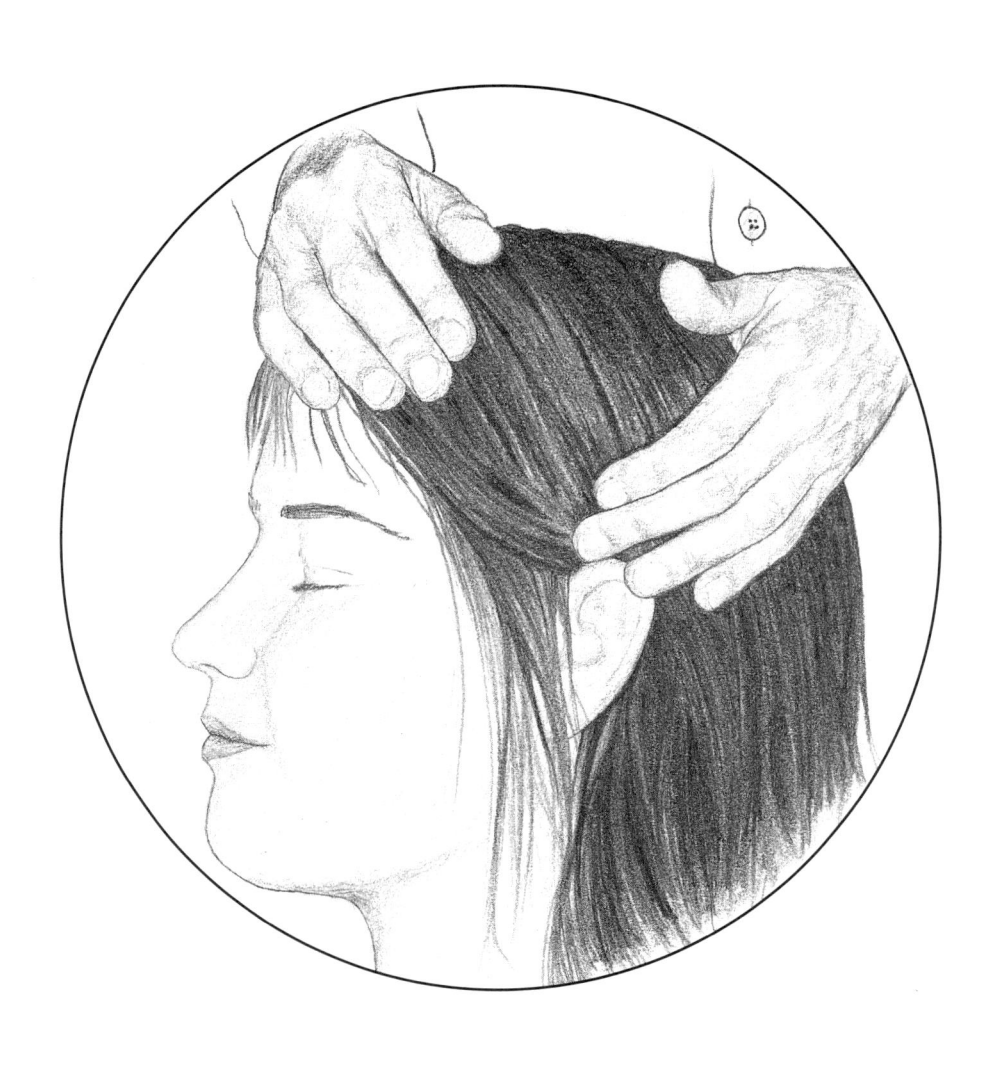

20 ...and across the base of the skull and up to the top of the ears (5–10 minutes or longer).

8. INTRODUCING THE PRACTICE

When introducing the Metamorphic Technique to children and adults with learning difficulties in the school or care setting, it may not always be appropriate nor indeed practical to begin by offering sessions of one hour duration in privacy.

Some people may initially prefer to receive shorter sessions and to receive them in social surroundings. Also, many staff have to work within the constraints of very limited resources and it is often necessary to meet individual needs for much of the time within a group context or at least be responsible for more than one person.

Due to the versatility of the technique, we can exercise a great deal of flexibility in making it available in a way that is not only appropriate from the point of view of the individual(s) concerned but, at the same time, is very practical.

Young children and some adults, for example, find it difficult to sit still for long periods and so the hour can be spread out during the course of the week, perhaps ten minutes each day. Some people may find receiving sessions of one hour duration from the start rather too invasive and possibly even distressing. In these circumstances, shorter sessions will of course be preferable.

In homes, people often like to receive sessions in their living room in the presence of others rather than in privacy and this can be done whilst they are watching television, listening to music, chatting to friends or simply sitting quietly.

The group context presents a very good way of introducing the technique to a number of people. Shorter sessions of 10-20 minutes duration can be offered, for example, as part of a relaxation session or offered to individuals alongside other quiet activities.

But how do we go about introducing the technique and still remain detached if we are to fulfill our role as catalysts? For if we were to decide who should receive sessions and for how long those sessions should last, then we would be in danger of imposing our will at the expense of the individual's own capacity for self-healing and creative growth.

The desire to help a particular individual may be very strong, especially when the person concerned is experiencing a great deal of difficulty in his life, but by stepping back and letting go of our desire to help, we are creating the space for the person to take responsibility whilst providing an opportunity for him to help himself.

We need to be clear about our motivation. Our role is simply to make the technique accessible and available to those who may wish to receive it. We act as catalysts and the desire for change must therefore originate from within the person himself. We can do this by ensuring that he is able to make an informed choice and that the practice is made available at the person's own pace.

An informed choice can be based upon the experience of observing a session taking place and/or receiving a "taster" session.

You may choose to demonstrate the technique by giving a session to another member of staff or a willing volunteer in your class or group. It is not necessary to formalise such an introduction as you will find that those who have a genuine interest will be drawn to it. For example, in a class of pupils aged between 6 and 8 years at a school for children with severe learning disabilities, sessions were offered to several of the children who expressed an interest as part of a weekly relaxation session. One autistic boy would initially retreat to the adjoining classroom toilet as soon as the sessions began, from where he would feel safe to observe the rest of the class from a distance. As the weeks progressed he would gradually leave the cubicle and get closer and closer to the rest of the group, until one day he put his bare foot upon the lap of a member of staff briefly before withdrawing to the toilet again. Eventually he requested to receive sessions each week and the class teacher commented that it was the only activity he really engaged in.

Sometimes it may take several weeks before anyone expresses any direct interest and, at other times, you may find people queuing up to receive sessions and very eager to place their feet upon your lap. So it is best to put aside any expectations.

Having experienced a session once, no matter how brief, the individual is then in a position to request a session at a later date if he or she wishes. How they go about it will vary from person to person of course and those with limited verbal abilities will discover their own way of making a request. This may, for example, take the form of kicking off their shoes, raising a big smile, giving direct and sustained eye contact or simply standing in close proximity to the staff member concerned.

When people do decide that they would like to receive a session, it is important to introduce it at their own individual pace. By allowing them to exercise their authority in determining the frequency and duration of the sessions received, we are enabling them to take responsibility for their own healing and growth process.

We therefore need to ensure that the recipient is able to communicate when he has had enough or to refuse completely (should he decide to change his mind). Even the most profoundly handicapped person is able to do this so long as we pay attention to his responses.

This may simply take the form of withdrawing the foot. When this occurs after you have worked on it for a while, then offer to do his other foot for about the same time to avoid feelings of lopsidedness. Usually people are happy to do so but, if not, then respect their choice.

In the case of individuals who are unable to move their feet easily, if at all, then it will be necessary to pay attention to their other means of communication. You need to ensure that they are in a position to make as direct a response as possible. For example, it may be preferable to sit them up rather than having them lying down, so that they can see what is being offered and respond accordingly, through facial expression or otherwise, to express their like or dislike of what is being provided as well as to indicate when they have had enough.

For example, I worked with one very timid young man who felt greatly reassured by the fact that the situation had been geared to ensure that he was in control. Initially, he would give a big grin when his feet were touched and, after a few minutes, he would begin to look uncomfortable and start to grimace which was when the session was brought to a close. In the following weeks the duration of the sessions gradually grew until he thoroughly enjoyed having his feet done for up to 45 minutes, often smiling throughout!

It is often the case that those who initially choose to receive shorter sessions on a regular basis will, after a number of sessions, express an increased willingness or indeed demand to receive sessions of longer duration.

When introducing this work to a group of adults with high support needs who attended a weekly relaxation session at a day centre, initially only one or two people expressed a willingness to have their feet done and then for only brief sessions. During the following weeks and months, the duration of sessions gradually increased as did the number of people who wished to receive sessions, until it became necessary to provide several hour–long sessions in a separate room. Such was the subsequent demand from clients in the rest of the centre that I have since been employed to provide sessions for six hours a week during the last four years. So don't feel disheartened by an initial lack of response. Big oak trees from little acorns grow!

Occasionally people may wish to ensure that their decision to refuse is fully respected. Consecutive refusals or willingness to accept only very brief sessions may be an indication that they are making sure that you do so. If so, pay attention to your motivation. Are you trying to help the person? Are you hoping to achieve a result?

It has been noticed that some very timid people will refuse on several occasions and will then later willingly request sessions by putting out their foot for you to touch, sometimes with great delight. Once they are satisfied that your motive is not to impose change upon them but to enable them to change for themselves, they will often gladly request sessions. It is as though their life-force is checking out that you are a true catalyst and will allow it to flow without restriction, with complete freedom.

For some people, particularly those with sensitive feet, touch on the feet may seem too invasive at first. In such circumstances, you can offer to work on their hands instead. After several weeks you may find that they are willing to receive sessions on the feet.

Work on the hands provides a good way of demonstrating what kind of contact is being offered thereby avoiding confusion that you may be offering something very different like cutting their toe nails or wishing to brush up on your chiropody skills!

Work on the hands is very convenient too because there are no shoes or socks to remove. From the point of view of the individual concerned, they offer a greater sense of control too because the hands are usually easier to offer and withdraw.

With very withdrawn people and those with multiple handicaps, it may be necessary to exercise particular restraint when introducing the technique for the first time. Many people with high support needs understandably feel very vulnerable about being touched. Touch can so often come to them in directional forms when they need lifting, dressing, feeding, bathing or toiletting and so touch can unintentionally become associated with promoting a sense of helplessness or lack of power. With the Metamorphic Technique, the emphasis is upon simply being with the person concerned.

It may therefore be necessary to spend five or ten minutes each week simply sitting alongside the person before offering sessions on the feet or hands. Bear in mind that the intention is not to persuade the person to accept sessions but to make the technique accessible by non–verbally communicating the uninvasive nature of what is being offered.

Some people may suddenly decide to cease the sessions or may not be interested at all and this of course needs to be totally respected. The prospect of change can be very threatening to some and they may prefer to remain in the security of their current situation for the time being until they feel ready to move on. When they do feel the need for change in their lives, they do at least know that the technique is available should they need it. The choice is theirs.

Providing sessions in a group context also opens up the possibility, where appropriate, for both children and adults to learn how to perform the technique themselves and this is explored in the next chapter.

9. DOING IT FOR THEMSELVES

The beauty of the Metamorphic Technique is its simplicity. What is more, no profound understanding of the underlying principles is required in order to perform it. It is a practice that can be easily learnt by both children and adults alike. Through discovering the ease with which they are able to learn the technique, they are afforded an empowering and fulfilling experience, as well as hopefully having a lot of fun along the way. From a practical standpoint, this allows your group to give and receive sessions themselves rather than relying wholly upon you and any other staff members involved.

Usually this shift from reliance upon staff towards taking increasing responsibility themselves occurs quite spontaneously and naturally where sessions are being provided regularly in a group context. Frequently, the group sessions are so enjoyed by pupils/clients and staff alike that the barriers between individuals begin to crumble giving rise to an increase in communication and openness.

Having experienced and observed a few sessions, some members of the group will begin to express a natural desire to offer the same to others in the group and will eventually simply get on with giving sessions, without prompting, to someone who is sat waiting. Conversely, those who are waiting to receive sessions may ask another group member to do their feet rather than continue waiting for a member of staff to be free.

I remember working with a small group of adults all of whom were rather shy and withdrawn. For several weeks I offered sessions to each member of the group for 15–20 minutes whilst the rest of the group were sat listening to some relaxing music. After several weeks, one woman spontaneously put her foot upon her neighbour's lap who then proceeded to rub it. This initiated a willingness by others to do the same until eventually most of the group were giving and receiving sessions on a regular basis and becoming very much more communicative whereas before they would sit much of the time in silence.

Some will be keen to learn through imitation whilst others will learn through their own discovery and natural sensitivity.

I tend to allow this process to occur naturally rather than control it or get bogged down with specific instruction. However, I do insist on two things. Firstly, that the giver and receiver sit at right angles to each other to convey an attitude of non-interference and, secondly, that the contact on the feet is gentle and not harsh but not so tentative as to be ticklish.

From this starting point, the individuals concerned can take on board as much or as little structure as they feel comfortable with. In groups, an actual demonstration can be provided informally simply by my offering sessions alongside the rest of the group, and often people are able to learn how to perform the technique in a matter of minutes. Others seem to need more time to feel confident and at ease with providing this kind of contact to the whole foot before expressing a desire to learn how to work on the specific areas of the feet (i.e. the spinal reflexes).

Every group member is different and it will consist of its own proportion of givers and receivers. Some will prefer to only give sessions whilst others choose only to receive. Many people like to both give and receive sessions. For some, sessions of 10–15 minutes duration are preferred whilst others like sessions to be much longer. Many people value the opportunity of giving and receiving sessions with different people in the group whilst others prefer to work with a particular friend. In either case this tendency needs to be respected totally.

In the past I have used oils when introducing this work to groups of children. I used to put a bottle fitted with a dropper lid in the centre of the group while we all sat together on mats. Those who felt like giving a session could then take a bottle and drop oil on their hands or the person's foot and proceed to rub the oil over the foot. It did provide a very useful way of starting the children off in learning how to rub the foot firmly enough to spread the oil over the foot (thereby avoiding ticklishness) and the nature of the oil would discourage any forceful grips! These days I find it unnecessary and regard oils as an avoidable burden because of all the mopping up required and so on. But do use oils if you wish.

Another useful aid that I have used with adult groups is a video camera. By compiling a collage of samples of pairs giving and receiving sessions in their own particular style and playing it back to the group, it provides a way of validating each individual's own unique approach and affirming the importance and value of allowing the fingers to move spontaneously in a way that is right for the person concerned. This provided the group with the confidence to begin to learn the specific practice of the Metamorphic Technique which provides a more defined structure within which the fingers can move around freely. Or as one young child put it: "You let your fingers do the walking".

Such videos have subsequently been borrowed by members of the group and used as a learning aid which led to some people providing sessions to their parents, carers, relatives and friends without any encouragement.

Using a video camera also enables the group members to focus upon their own resources and sensitivity in learning the technique. For example, in one group of adults who were giving and receiving sessions, a newcomer came into the room to join the group whilst I was filming. He had never before observed or experienced a session. He sat next to a woman who was lying down waiting to have her feet done. Initially he looked rather vague and hesitant as he put his hands upon her feet. He seemed to be looking to me for guidance and direction as to what to do next but I was unable to provide this as I was too busy filming. Then the person lying down told him to "Get on with it then", whilst he focussed upon his hands. After a couple of minutes, he began to rub her foot and soon spontaneously started to work up and down the spinal reflexes!

Some people will of course prefer a more structured approach and I have displayed charts in these cases. Watercolour marker pens can also be used to demonstrate the location of the spinal reflexes for those who require it. A few have asked me to compile a small manual of the reflexes of the feet, hands and head for use as a learning aid which they have reported to have found very useful. Some have used them to do their own feet before retiring to bed. This idea has since led to the production of a more comprehensive manual complete with illustrations and diagrams.

People will often do their feet when there is no-one else around to do them and I have noticed this particularly in groups of odd numbers. One young man at a day centre who had come to a group session for a few weeks and then later chose to receive fortnightly individual sessions with me, was found in the room I use to provide sessions performing the technique accurately on a day that I was not at the centre. It demonstrated on the one hand that he was now wishing to receive sessions on a more frequent basis, but it also showed he had taken responsibility by getting on and doing them himself. It is usually preferable to have someone do your feet for you but it is certainly better to do your own feet than not at all.

After introducing work on the feet, then work on the hands and head can also be learnt.

When sessions are over, don't forget to remind people to wash their hands in cold water.

21 Doing it for oneself

And whilst all this giving and receiving of sessions is going on, remember to include yourself. What better way of creating opportunities for others to learn than by sitting back and enjoying having your feet done?

10. CONCLUSION

Attitudes towards people with learning disabilities are changing. Rather than employing rigid structures to control and contain people in institutions separated from the rest of the population, there is now increasing emphasis upon facilitating the development of the individual in the community, calling for a more flexible and creative approach. Indeed, it is this focus upon the individual that lies at the heart of the current changes.

The Metamorphic Technique has a unique and valuable contribution to make to the facilitation of this process because it enables people to discover their true individuality by creating a means by which they are able to become aware of their own needs and resources.

As members of staff, we are continually seeking to create new opportunities for our pupils and clients so that they might be able to realise their full potential, which has led to the discovery and use of new and more appropriate approaches.

My findings indicate that the Metamorphic Technique, due to its simplicity, versatility and accessibility, as well as its empowering qualities, has an important contribution to make in the area of personal growth for both children and adults with learning disabilities and is well-suited for use in the education, health and social services where meeting the needs of the individual forms the basis of service provision.

Its potential, like that of the individuals we work with, is considerable.

FURTHER INFORMATION

THE METAMORPHIC ASSOCIATION

The Metamorphic Association, a registered charity, was created in 1979 to help promote Metamorphosis by providing instruction to the public generally by conducting classes and workshops, individual tuition and lectures to interested groups. It maintains a register of members and offers a referral service. It also provides for an exchange of information to members and to the public generally through the Journal, Programme and various publications.

Membership is open to all practitioners with the necessary training and experience. Practitioners who do not wish to become members, and non-practitioners, can become "Friends of the Association".

For details of training and other publications on the Metamorphic Technique contact:

The Metamorphic Association
67, Ritherdon Road,
Tooting,
LONDON
SW17 8QE
Tel and Fax: 0181 672 5951

Further copies of *Becoming Who We Are* are available from the Metamorphic Association and from the Author direct at the address below (please include 75p P&P).

Workshop organisers and enquirers can contact the Author at:–

**David Singer,
11, Roseberry Terrace,
Frieze Hill,
TAUNTON,
Somerset
TA1 1EZ**

Tel: (01823) 334530